JB YEO

Stair, Nancy.

Michelle Yeoh /

9x 9/03 LT 5/03

12x4/15 LT 3/11   CHAVEZ-J

Martial Arts Masters

Michelle Yeoh

Nancy L. Stair

The Rosen Publishing Group, Inc.
New York

For Babette and Lee
thanks for everything—
especially Charley

Published in 2002 by The Rosen Publishing Group, Inc.
29 East 21st Street, New York, NY 10010

First Edition

Library of Congress Cataloging-in-Publication Data

Stair, Nancy.
Michelle Yeoh / by Nancy L. Stair—1st ed.
p. cm. — (Martial arts masters)
Includes bibliographical references and index.
ISBN 0-8239-3520-5 (library binding)
1. Yeoh, Michelle, 1963– 2. Motion picture actors and
actresses—Malaysia—Biography. 3. Martial artists—
Malaysia—Biography. I. Title. II. Series.
PN2960.M3 S73 2002
791.43'028'092—dc21

2001004611

Manufactured in the United States of America

Table of Contents

Michelle Yeoh poses with her waxwork double at Madame Tussaud's Wax Museum in Hong Kong. Her success in film has made her one of the most popular actresses in Asia.

Michelle Yeoh's story may seem like a fairy tale: She floated from a privileged childhood in Malaysia, to schools in London, to the glamour of the dance world, to acting. She is famous throughout Asia and now America.

But like anyone else in this world, Yeoh had to work hard to achieve her goals. She spent years training as a dancer and took many small roles in low-quality films to gain acting experience.

She suffered numerous injuries as a stuntwoman and endured the pain of rehabilitation as she recovered. All her hard work has paid off: Yeoh is now the most watched actress in Asia and a rising star worldwide, commanding an estimated $13 million per picture.

Michelle Yeoh is aware of the impact she has had on her audiences over the course of her career. Her simple yet profound choice to perform her own stunts broke new ground for Asian actresses. Michelle Yeoh's hard work and willingness to take risks should be an inspiration to all of us.

Chapter 1

Michelle Yeoh's Early Years

On screen, Michelle Yeoh sometimes looks fierce and arrogant, like the mythological Chinese warriors she so often portrays. In real life, she is the sweet beauty queen she was as a young woman. Her voice is soft, and her accent is part British boarding school and part Malaysian childhood.

Michelle Yeoh was born Yeoh Chu-Keng on August 6, 1962, in the Malaysian town of Ipoh, where tin mining, palm oil farming, and rubber production are the main industries. Her father worked as a lawyer and her mother is a homemaker. Her family still lives in Malaysia. This includes her father, Kian Geik, age seventy-six, and her mother, Janet, sixty-one. She has a younger brother, Bobby, thirty-three, who is married to a woman from Hong Kong and has three children.

As a schoolgirl, Yeoh excelled at almost every sport, especially squash, diving, and swimming. She also enjoyed rugby, which must have been a sign of her future taste for the rough-and-tumble world of action movies. Yeoh once said of her childhood that she had no responsibilities or worries, just good friends and family. She enjoyed weekend fishing trips to

Pangkor Island, and still tells friends of the time she caught a thirty-pound snapper.

That childhood built a strong foundation for Yeoh. She is still close to the people she grew up with—one of her childhood friends, Philip Hemnell, now accompanies her on every film, working as her personal assistant. He is a former investment banker who decided Wall Street wasn't for him. Hemnell, who is half-Chinese and half-British, met Yeoh when they were both ten years old. Her house was next door to the Ipoh Swimming Club, and her family always kept an open door for anyone who wanted to escape the Malaysian heat.

In Ipoh, Yeoh grew up speaking English and Malay, with some Chinese lessons thrown in on the

Michelle Yeoh stands by a portrait of herself taken when she was fourteen years old. The portrait was intended to launch the search for an actress to play the part of Michelle as a teenager in a film called *The Touch*.

weekends. When she moved to Hong Kong, she learned enough Chinese for conversation and for speaking lines of dialogue, but she never mastered the written language. (Hong Kong action films are usually in Chinese.) Later, as an actor on the set, assistants would read her lines of dialogue and she would memorize them.

From Dancing to Acting

Michelle Yeoh was a tomboy, always on the move and playing with her brother's friends. By the age of four she was taking ballet classes. Her dance training would later prove to be a tremendous asset. "Every little girl should have the opportunity to have ballet training because it teaches you such control of your body,"

Yeoh said. Eventually, she began to dream of becoming a dancer.

After finishing high school, she studied ballet at the Royal Academy of Dance in London. She graduated with a bachelor of arts degree in dance and choreography and went back to Malaysia to spend time with her family. Then she returned to England to work on her master's degree in dance. She had injured her back dancing, and although it was not a serious injury, it would hamper her career as a ballerina. Instead, she planned to become a choreographer.

That she became an actress has surprised Michelle Yeoh more than anyone else. Throughout her school years, she wanted only to be a dancer. "Twelve years ago, if someone had come up to me and said, 'One day you are going to be an actress,' I would have laughed my head off," Yeoh said. "I had always wanted to be a dancer, I had always wanted to be a choreographer, I had always wanted to be a teacher, anything to do with dance." Although she had minored in drama to enhance the expression in her dance, she had no plans whatsoever to act.

When she returned home in 1982, her mother and some of her friends played a little trick on Yeoh—they secretly entered her in the 1983 Miss Malaysia pageant. They thought that the experience would be good for her. But she surpassed everyone's expectations by winning. What seemed like a minor diversion ended up completely changing the direction of her life.

Yeoh reigned as Miss Malaysia for a year, touring the country and seeing the world. She also received plenty of notice from the public. After her year was up, a friend who knew Yeoh from her tour as a beauty queen recommended her for a national TV commercial.

This was not just any commercial: its star was none other than Hong Kong action-film star Jackie Chan, the hottest actor in Hong Kong! Chan is now known worldwide as one of the greatest action-film stars since Bruce Lee, but in 1983 he was famous mostly in Asia, which comprised some two billion people—half the world's population. For Michelle Yeoh, costarring with Jackie Chan—even in a watch commercial—was as big an opportunity as anyone could hope for.

Hong Kong Cinema

The term "Hong Kong action film" evolved in Asia from the mid 1980s to the mid 1990s. It is a blanket term for most of the action movies produced in Hong Kong. These movies can be police stories, period epics, ghost stories, martial arts comedies, and even Hollywood-style blockbusters. They can be silly and outrageous, funny and violent.

In Hong Kong films, there are good guys and bad guys, honor-bound codes of chivalry, and sappy love stories with happy endings. But most of all, there is a tendency in Hong Kong action cinema to throw in everything but the kitchen sink. These movies are often filled with inventive stunts, slapstick, screwball comedy, mistaken identities, dreamy musical interludes, hand-to-hand combat, love, honor, the old double-cross, car chases, occasional R-rated romance, and every other cinematic idea ever created. It seems chaotic, but these movies are made with a light touch that keeps the plots from ever getting bogged down.

An interesting piece of trivia about all of these films is that no matter what language the actors seem to be speaking, you'll see that their lips don't always match the sounds coming out of them. That's because Hong Kong action films are often shot without sound—dialogue is dubbed in later. This enables the film production crew to work quickly in otherwise noisy locations, and it helps with the final destinations of these films, which are dubbed in many dialects for audiences throughout the world.

Viewers may have to adjust their thinking to accept the quirks of the Hong Kong film industry, which is very different from that of Hollywood. Subtitled films often have the added dimension of sometimes questionable and bizarre translations, which is all part of the fun of Hong Kong action films.

The commercial's producers were impressed by Yeoh's natural acting ability and her obvious grace as a trained dancer. Not only did she get the commercial, they offered her a film contract for two years. Fame was right around the corner. And so was Dickson Poon.

Dickson Poon is a Hong Kong entrepreneur who used a $900,000 loan from his parents to build a multimillion-dollar retail empire. In the 1980s, he formed a production company, D&B Films, and began to experiment in filmmaking. Poon was one of the producers who cast Michelle Yeoh in the watch commercial with Jackie Chan. Soon, Poon and Yeoh were dating, and Yeoh began her acting career.

Chapter 2

Making the Leap into Movies

ichelle Yeoh played a social
worker in her first movie,
Owl vs. Dumbo (1984).
Although her role in this comedy was
minor, it was enough to whet her
appetite for acting in movies. It
wasn't much of a part, but it was her
film debut. Like anyone else, even
stars have to start small.

Her second film, 1985's *Yes,
Madam!* was a personal breakthrough.

Under the direction of Corey Yuen, she and American martial arts film star Cynthia Rothrock play a pair of cops looking for microfilm that will enable them to take down some of Hong Kong's toughest gangsters. The D&B producers realized that, with her extensive dance training and athletic background, Yeoh could be leaping, kicking, and slugging just like one of the boys. For her part, Yeoh was determined not to be just another beauty queen who needed a double for her stunts. She felt that the audience needed to see an actor performing the action of the character, not a faraway shot of someone who looked similar. Furthermore, she realized that to survive in the male-dominated world of Hong Kong action films, she needed to hit hard and be willing to get hit back.

Doing Her Own Stunts

Before she worked in Hong Kong action films, Michelle Yeoh thought that the stunts and fighting in these movies were all faked. But filming *Yes, Madam!* changed her perspective. One day on the set, she watched the director shoot a fight sequence. When it was over, one actor was on the floor, doubled over in pain.

Ever the thrill-seeker, Yeoh found it strange that someone else should do her stunts. "I remember the very first movie I did, I used to stand there and think, he can do it, why can't I?" she said. "He hasn't got an extra arm or an extra leg. It's physically possible." Yeoh jumped at the opportunity to learn how to do stunt work. She saw it as her ticket to a film career. In addition, she

Yeoh's willingness to perform her own stunts helped to advance her acting career. Here, she performs a stunt jump with Pierce Brosnan in *Tomorrow Never Dies*.

loved doing the dangerous work—
she got a rush diving from three
stories and riding in speeding cars.

Even with a taste for danger and
challenge, Yeoh had obstacles to
overcome in learning the craft of
stunt martial arts for *Yes, Madam!*
After all, she was a dancer, not a
fighter. The stunt doubles on the set
were skeptical about her abilities.
But they changed their minds after
Yeoh proved her fearlessness with
her first stunt. "I did the most
ungraceful flip and just went splat,"
Yeoh said. "After that, they thought,
'OK, she's one of us.'"

Yeoh's evolution from dancer to
action film star required hard work
and dedication. To train for her role,
she put in eight-hour days working
out at the gym. She already had the
discipline and training to learn and

execute difficult moves. Her training in dance gave her the physical strength and mental focus needed to master stunts. "Action is really just choreography," Yeoh said. "You and your partners know exactly where you need to move so that it looks beautiful and so nobody gets hurt." Of course, there are differences in the types of moves being choreographed, but ultimately, the amount of dedication and determination is the same.

For fighting scenes, Yeoh learned combinations of several different kinds of martial arts techniques, and she still often borrows from many disciplines. In many contemporary Hong Kong action films, there is no particular type of combat style that is required. Directors and audiences want fast, exciting, and death-defying action. Generally, action heroes and heroines employ whatever fighting techniques they need to get themselves out of a jam—from kung fu to modern-day street fighting.

Whereas films in the United States are coordinated so that no one actually gets hurt, Hong Kong action films include real fighting—and real pain. The audience must remember that the actors in Hong Kong action films do not work with blue screens or green screens, as do many Hollywood action stars. Blue screens hang behind the actor in the studio. As the camera rolls, the actor mimes the action; for instance, writhing at the end of a rope. An image is later projected onto the blue or green screen showing footage that makes the actor appear to be dangling off a building, when in fact he or she is safely in the studio, standing in front

Pierce Brosnan and Michelle Yeoh perform a stunt motorcycle ride during the filming of *Tomorrow Never Dies* in Bangkok, Thailand.

of a screen. Hong Kong action movies use few or no digital effects, so the breathtaking scenes of rushing trains, diving helicopters, and speeding bikes are real. The actors really *do* the action; it is not created by computer special effects like in most Hollywood pictures.

Doing stunts in Hong Kong action movies can be dangerous work. If an actor doesn't hit his or her marks during a scene, or doesn't do exactly what has been rehearsed, he or she can throw off the other actors. And when the other actors are wielding knives and flying through the air kicking at head-level, being in the wrong place at the wrong time can be a problem. An actor has to throw his or her punches exactly as he or she has rehearsed, or someone could be seriously hurt.

Doing stunts in Hong Kong action movies requires not just the ability to execute martial arts moves. There is a certain type of dramatic acting that goes along with the movements. Yeoh spent hours in front of a mirror practicing aggressive facial expressions. "You could be throwing a hard punch," she said, "but if your face doesn't say, 'I'm going to kill this guy,' the audience is not impressed."

Yeoh's hard work and training for *Yes, Madam!* paid off. In the film, she performed the stunt that jump-started her career: Sitting on a glass-enclosed balcony when two thugs came at her with knives, she flipped backward, smashing through the glass. Famous Hollywood director Quentin Tarantino has said that, to this day, he can recite each of Yeoh's moves from that scene. The stunt put her on the map, and she's been a presence in Hong Kong action films ever since.

After *Yes Madam!*, Yeoh had a bit part in Jackie Chan's *Twinkle Twinkle Lucky Stars* in 1985. The two performers had worked together for one day a year earlier shooting the watch commercial. But you could hardly say they were working together again: Chan was the film's star, while Yeoh had a tiny cameo as a judo instructor. They never even crossed paths during the film shoot. Neither could have imagined it at the time, but they would one day team up to star in a blockbuster Hong Kong action film.

Twinkle Twinkle Lucky Stars was a success in Hong Kong, making HK$28 million at the box office. It was another impressive entry on Yeoh's résumé.

Michelle Yeoh on Stunts

I think you should always have that "double-take" moment. You should always be afraid, aware and very respectful when you're doing stunts and action. I am very careful about what I do, but I could never prevent an accident. No one can. So I make sure I work with the best stunt team, because it's all about collaboration. It's not about one person being brave enough to do it. It's about everything coming together, then you just hope and pray that everything is safely done by the end of the day. The big stunts are always managed. It's always the little things that create chaos. But if you are gifted and you've done years and years of stunts, then they come to you more naturally.

—in *Venice* magazine

In 1986, she won her first starring role in *In the Line of Duty* (also distributed under the title *Royal Warriors*). Her fight scenes were truly remarkable and groundbreaking for a female action star. But the film was only a modest success, grossing some HK$14.5 million. In 1987, Yeoh had a noncombat role in *Easy Money.* Also in 1987, she starred in the low-budget (and low-grossing) *Magnificent Warriors*. With a handful of films under her belt, she was on her way to becoming the first female action star in Hong Kong cinema. It seemed nothing could steer her off-course.

Retirement

In 1988, Yeoh shocked her fans by marrying Dickson Poon and abruptly retiring from making movies. Rumors circulated that Poon had asked her to end her career, but Yeoh denied it: "No one can make me do anything I don't want to do," she said.

In retirement, Yeoh gradually morphed into what is referred to in Hong Kong as a *tai tai*—a married woman of leisure. Yeoh became a fixture of Hong Kong's fashion boutiques and society pages. But after a couple of years, she got bored with a life devoted only to shopping and partying. Yeoh felt unfulfilled. She was young, talented, and beautiful, and she wanted to have a career of her own in dance or film. She had already proven herself capable, and she certainly had the drive to succeed.

But Poon flatly refused to allow his wife to work. One of Yeoh's friends told an interviewer, "[Yeoh] became bored and fed up. She would go shopping virtually every day, then come home with six bags and throw them in a corner and cry." Yeoh's private life was beginning to disintegrate. She gradually came to resent her husband. Yeoh and Poon divorced after three years of marriage.

Neither Yeoh, Poon, nor any of their friends will comment on the exact reasons for the breakup. Soon after the divorce, Poon dissolved his film company. He has since remarried and now has two children.

Out of Retirement, Onto Fame

No longer a lady of leisure, Yeoh quickly went back to making movies. She was itching to return to her career, which had been on hold during her marriage. Her fans in Hong Kong were happy that the first action heroine was going to make movies again. Jackie Chan offered her a part in his film *Police Story 3: Super Cop,* and she grabbed it. In it, she plays a security chief who teams up with a Hong Kong detective (played by

Michelle Yeoh starred as Inspector Yang in *Police Story 3: Super Cop,* the film that marked her acting comeback.

Chan) to break up an international drug ring.

Hong Kong cinema had become popular in the United States and Canada in the early 1990s, and Yeoh's amazing stunt abilities were showcased in *Police Story 3: Super Cop*. She impressed audiences and movie producers all over the world. For Yeoh, *Police Story 3: Super Cop* was both a comeback and a breakthrough. This and each successive film drew her closer to the ultimate dream of many actors around the world: making it to Hollywood.

Chapter 3

The Road to Stardom

*P*olice Story 3: Super Cop would show whether years of shopping had blunted Yeoh's capabilities and courage. It was the third installment of Jackie Chan's enormously popular *Police Story* films and was much anticipated by audiences. Best of all, it would pair Yeoh with star Jackie Chan. Chan was looking forward to working with Yeoh again after the watch commercial they made together at the very start of her career. Yeoh was certainly looking forward to working with Chan, the top star in Hong Kong action cinema, and at the time a rising star in the United States and Canada. Moviegoers throughout Asia would flock to see their hero Chan, and the exposure would be valuable for Yeoh's career. She would appear in magazines throughout Asia to promote the film. Many movie producers would see her, too—including Hollywood producers. This kind of exposure would not only help her make a comeback, but it would boost her career as a movie actor.

In the movie, Chan and Yeoh go undercover in China to break up a crime syndicate. Their assignment ends with a chase involving Chan leaping from a building to a rope ladder dangling from a helicopter and Yeoh jumping from a motorcycle onto a moving train.

The film's director, Stanley Tong, was himself a stuntman and wanted to break the unwritten rule of martial arts films by teaming a stuntman with a stuntwoman. "Never before in a Jackie Chan movie can you see a girl who can fight," he said. "It became competitive, and the film benefits because you're not just seeing him; you're seeing another action star who's female and they're both raising each other up one notch." Throughout the movie, Yeoh and Chan do their own stunts, and they make their death-defying moves seem frighteningly realistic. That's what being a successful action-movie star is all about.

Inspector Yang (Michelle Yeoh) kicks a bad guy in the head in *Police Story 3: Super Cop*.

At the beginning of the shoot, Chan was skeptical as to whether women could fight, preferring them to look pretty and support his role in a film. By the end, he was legitimately concerned that he might be upstaged. By doing her own stunts, Michelle Yeoh had brought another dimension to the typical Jackie Chan movie. "When Stanley approached me, I said, 'Look, you have to promise me that I'm not just going to be the normal Jackie Chan girl,'" she said. Yeoh is the only woman that Chan has ever allowed to do her own stunts. In fact, he allowed Yeoh many opportunities to display her astounding skills. In some ways, she steals the movie. Her action fight scenes benefit from her years of ballet training: while exciting, they are also choreographed and graceful.

In one scene, Yeoh leaps onto a moving truck and holds on to the sides as it goes whizzing through traffic. Eventually she is able to flip on to the top of the truck. The bad guys inside start shooting through the roof with a machine gun. This forces her to leap backwards—falling off the truck and on to the top of the car behind her, driven by Chan.

The final stunt with the motorcycle is performed again by Yeoh. It is amazing in its own right, but even more so when you realize that she had never ridden a motorcycle before making this film. After she learned how to ride a motorcycle, she then

Jackie Chan

Jackie Chan was born on April 7, 1954, in Hong Kong under the given name Chan Kwong Sang, meaning "born in Hong Kong." He was the son of a desperately poor couple who could barely raise the money for the hospital bill and were almost forced to sell him to the delivering doctor.

When Jackie was seven years old, his family moved to Australia. His father sent Jackie to the Peking Opera Research Institute. Students at the academy had regular schooling in addition to learning kung fu, stunts, flips, and somersaults.

From the age of seven, Jackie's life was dedicated to the institute. He studied Chinese opera and worked at the institute some eighteen hours a day. Along with six other pupils, he performed an opera called *Seven Little Fortunes,* a name which would also be given to their group. The Seven Little Fortunes staged public performances at other venues throughout Hong Kong.

But times were changing, and interest in Chinese opera was declining. Audiences preferred Hong Kong action films, which were becoming very popular throughout

Asia. The Seven Little Fortunes and the other opera students were loaned out to work as stuntmen in the burgeoning Hong Kong film industry.

At the age of seventeen, Jackie left the institute to work full-time as a movie stunt-man. Soon, he was doing stunts for the famous action star Bruce Lee in movies such as *Fist of Fury* and *Enter the Dragon*.

Eventually, Jackie developed his own style of acting, a comedic exaggeration of the typical martial arts film. He made many popular films, including the phenomenal *Police Story* series in the 1980s and 1990s. He also collaborated with his stunt "brothers" Sammo Hung, Yuen Wah, and Yuen Biao in many movies, including *Project A, My Lucky Stars*, and *Dragons Forever*.

Jackie tried to break into Hollywood in the early 1980s, with disappointing results. He made another attempt in the mid 1990s. Acting in his own comic style in 1995's *Rumble in the Bronx* and 1997's *Mr. Nice Guy*, he became popular in the United States. But it was the film *Rush Hour* in 1999 that got the most attention from American audiences. Jackie Chan became the first Hong Kong action star to make it in Hollywood.

had to do the stunt: drive the bike up an inclined ramp, jump twenty feet into space, land on the moving train, and stop the motorcycle before it flew off the train. "I must have been crazy," she later said of the scene.

Police Story 3: Super Cop was a massive success, the highest grossing film in Asia in 1992, making Michelle Yeoh the highest-paid actress in Asia. The film ended up being a breakthrough role for her in a multitude of ways. She proved to audiences all over the world that even though she had been gone for a few years, she still had what it took to be a great stuntwoman and actress. After five years in retirement, Yeoh looked better and more confident than ever. She was stronger, lovelier, more graceful and mature as an actress, and had a real charisma

Michelle Yeoh and Jackie Chan attend a party at Planet Hollywood in New York City to celebrate the U.S. premiere of *Police Story 3: Super Cop*.

about her that was not as evident in her earlier films.

Yeoh spent the next several years learning the ropes in Hong Kong action cinema and honing her stunt skills, becoming a star in her own right. She would eventually set her sights on the ultimate career move for an actor: Hollywood.

Chapter 4

Coming to America

Michelle Yeoh's career came roaring back after her show-stopping performance in *Police Story 3: Super Cop,* where she matched Jackie Chan stunt for stunt. She made such a strong impression in that film that her character went solo for *Police Story 4,* with Jackie Chan making a cameo appearance in drag.

Yeoh's career took off. Whether she was wielding a sword or jumping a motorcycle onto a speeding train, her intensity and flair burned brightly in her successive movies. In 1993 alone, she made *Executioners, Butterfly & Sword, Holy Weapon, Once a Cop,* and *Tai Chi Master.* She played Ching, the invisible woman, in *The Heroic Trio* and its sequel *Executioners,* where she was part of a superheroine trio with other Hong Kong superstars Maggie Cheung and Anita Mui.

She played another strong-willed heroine in 1994's *Wing Chun,* showing that a tofu saleswoman in medieval China could be just as tough as a modern-day cop. Another memorable action movie was 1994's *Wonder Seven.* Beyond the action arena, Yeoh was able to show her dramatic force in 1996's *Ah Kam: The Story of a Stuntwoman* and in 1997's *The Soong Sisters.*

In *Wing Chun*, Michelle Yeoh plays a woman who successfully defends her village against a band of robbers.

Yeoh was by far the most famous and well-paid actress in Hong Kong cinema. When Hong Kong cinema became popular in the United States and Canada in the early 1990s, Yeoh's amazing train stunt in *Police Story 3* was an image that audiences—and producers—remembered.

From Hong Kong to Hollywood

Hollywood producers Michael G. Wilson and Barbara Broccoli were seeking an actress to play opposite Pierce Brosnan (playing James Bond, Agent 007) in *Tomorrow Never Dies*, the most recent installment of the popular James Bond series. Bond girls have traditionally been sexy, gorgeous, a little helpless, and in need of rescue by Bond. But Wilson and Broccoli weren't looking for just another Bond bimbo. They wanted a woman who could hold her own with Agent 007. They were looking for an actress to be the Bond girl of the twenty-first century. Who better than Michelle Yeoh?

In 1996, Yeoh had taken a trip to Los Angeles, where she made the rounds in Hollywood, networking and meeting important people who could help her get roles. (Being successful in many professions requires not only skills, but knowing people who can help you get good jobs.) She met Jeff Kleeman, a producer at United Artists, who thought she would be perfect in a Bond movie.

While casting *Tomorrow Never Dies,* he remembered Yeoh and

Already the most successful actress in Hong Kong, Michelle Yeoh's career fortune rose even higher when she became a Bond girl.

called her to audition. She would be reading opposite Pierce Brosnan himself! It was a nerve-racking experience for Yeoh, but producer Broccoli kindly arranged a dinner for her to meet the actor the night before. They quickly hit it off, and their chemistry showed in the screen test. Yeoh was about to become the next Bond girl. The role catapulted her onto Hollywood's radar screen. It was her international debut, and it would make her a star.

A Bond Girl for the New Millennium

Yeoh more than proved James Bond's equal, even getting her own solo fight scene without 007—a first for any Bond girl. She was celebrated as the first woman to keep pace with James Bond. "In the old days, the Bond girl was the blonde girl in the swimming pool. We're going into the twenty-first century and women are not just gorgeous to look at but smart. They're intelligent and just as smart as Bond," Yeoh said.

In the film, Yeoh plays Wai Lin, an agent of the People's External Security Force in Beijing. She strikes up an unlikely partnership with James Bond, an agent of Her Majesty's Secret Service, and they join forces to battle an evil media mogul. In one sequence, the accidental allies get handcuffed together, then share a wild motorcycle ride through the crowded streets and across the rooftops of an Asian city.

Tomorrow Never Dies represented many firsts: It was Michelle Yeoh's

As the rough-and-tumble Colonel Wai Lin in *Tomorrow Never Dies*, Michelle Yeoh revolutionized the role of the Bond girl.

first big Hollywood film, the first time a Bond girl had stunts of her own, and the first time an actress in a Hollywood movie had done such extensive stunts. Often, insurance companies will not allow actors to do their own stunts in movies; the cost of insuring them against their value to the movie studio is simply too expensive. But the producers realized that Yeoh was a hard act to follow as a stuntwoman: her doubles didn't come close to the original! Yeoh wound up doing many of her own stunts; in fact, she did virtually everything that wasn't strictly prohibited by the producers' insurance policy.

Tomorrow Never Dies was wildly popular, grossing $218 million overseas and $125.2 million in the United States, for a total of

$343.2 million, according to www.boxofficeguru.com.

The importance of being cast as a Bond girl cannot be overstated: It can help build an actress's career, or it can sink it. Hollywood veterans often speak of the Bond girl curse: After appearing as a Bond girl, some actresses are never able to break out of the mold. But talk of the Bond girl curse or the "short career span of beauty queens" failed to deter Yeoh. A big Hollywood blockbuster like *Tomorrow Never Dies* has the power of making a solid impression of an actor in the minds of audiences around the world. *Super Cop* made Michelle Yeoh a star in Asia, but being in a Bond movie increased her popularity around the world. *Tomorrow Never Dies* put Michelle Yeoh on the map internationally.

Michelle Yeoh was the first Bond girl to be portrayed as an equal to Agent 007.

Her Next Move

You might think that, having established a foothold in Hollywood, Yeoh would stay there to try to capitalize on her new fame. But for her next major role, she returned to China to act in director Ang Lee's Mandarin-language epic *Crouching Tiger, Hidden Dragon,* set during the reign of the nineteenth century Qing Dynasty. The film's stunts—especially those staged high atop roofs and in trees—are visually stunning.

Yeoh stars as Yu Shu Lien, a renowned swordfighter who tutors a headstrong female martial-arts prodigy, Jen (Zhang Ziyi), and balances her professional obligations with her attraction to a fellow warrior, played by Chow Yun Fat.

Yeoh was on a publicity tour for *Tomorrow Never Dies* when she met Ang Lee. She was the first actor whom he approached to do the film, and she was sold on the idea immediately. She was familiar with Lee's work and had always admired him—particularly the way he handles his actors and his sensitivity to his cast and crew. In addition, she wanted to do more than just action films. She wanted to grow as an actor, doing more than action for action's sake. After she read the script, Yeoh thought she would find the perfect balance between action and acting in *Crouching Tiger, Hidden Dragon*. She was right.

Chapter 5

Joy and Pain

*C*rouching Tiger, Hidden *Dragon* was an incredibly successful movie, popular with critics and audiences alike. Especially important, at least for Michelle Yeoh, was that it was a hit in the United States. In fact, it was the first foreign film in history to earn more than $100 million in the United States. It grossed $81 million overseas and $127.4 million in the United States, for a total of $208.4 million worldwide, according to www.boxofficeguru.com. These aren't even the final numbers: The film will make even more money on video and DVD.

Crouching Tiger, Hidden Dragon was nominated for ten Academy Awards, the most nominations ever for a foreign film. Yeoh even went to

Crouching Tiger, Hidden Dragon won Academy Awards for cinematography, original score, and art/set direction, as well as the award for the best foreign film.

Los Angeles on March 25, 2001, to be an Academy Awards presenter. There were about one billion people around the world watching her and seeing clips of her in the film.

Action-film fans in the West finally got to see Yeoh's range as both a stuntwoman and an actor. It put her in a position to demand better—and more lucrative—roles.

Fighting Pain and Injury

But for all its rewards, *Crouching Tiger* was Yeoh's most difficult shoot ever. She suffered a series of injuries (both minor and major) on various sets over the years. Yeoh's career of high-flying stunts has resulted in the occasional dislocated shoulder and broken rib, but in 1995, while shooting *Ah Kam: The Story of a*

helle Yeoh and Chow Yun Fat arrive on stage to present
award for best visual effects during the Academy Awards
emony in Los Angeles, California, on March 25, 2001.

Stuntwoman, she suffered a serious injury. She misjudged a jump off an eighteen-foot wall and landed on her head, cracking a vertebra. She was put in traction, and it was feared that she would never walk again. Yet within a month, she was back on the set as if nothing had happened.

Putting together a movie can take years. The producers have to raise money, usually tens of millions of dollars. This is spent on hiring other people to do the many jobs needed to make a film. *Crouching Tiger, Hidden Dragon* had taken two years to bring together, even before shooting began. The cast and crew had been assembled and were working together in Hong Kong, Beijing, and Taiwan to make director Lee's dream a reality. Filming had finally begun. But

Michelle Yeoh as Yu Shu Lien in *Crouching Tiger, Hidden Dragon*

while filming the very first action sequence, Yeoh suffered a fall and injured her left knee.

Yeoh had been shooting a fight scene late into the night. As a result of a minor mistiming in the sequence, she landed incorrectly and her leg collapsed under her. Yeoh tore her anterior cruciate ligament (ACL). Her knee was swollen and inflamed, and she was in excruciating pain. Tearing an ACL is usually a season-ending or even career-ending injury for college athletes and professional athletes. But Yeoh had a movie to finish. "You go into self-denial," Yeoh said. "You hope it's a sprain, but when you turn right and your knee is swinging left, you know it's not normal." With his star suffering from a torn ligament, Ang Lee's

Wire Work

Many Hong Kong action movies are "period pictures" (movies set in a particular historical period). Directors of these films prefer their actors to use specific fighting techniques that are historically accurate to the time in which the movie is set. For example, in Chinese culture, many mythical martial arts figures could fly. In a famous scene from *Crouching Tiger, Hidden Dragon,* two cloaked figures fly across rooftops, leap softly to the ground thirty feet below, and glide back up with fearless speed, hesitating in midair as if they are defying the laws of gravity. They move with mystical grace. They seem otherworldly, like kung fu fighting apparitions.

One of the figures is Michelle Yeoh. Although these mythical characters being portrayed onscreen can fly, the mortals playing them can't do it without wires. Wire work is very much a part of the Hong Kong film culture; Michelle Yeoh's predecessors in martial arts cinema have been doing wire work for generations and are masters of the craft. But wire work is risky business. "Actually it is not fun," Yeoh said. "Because you are just strapped into a corset the whole time and you have no control of your movements. But you are hanging there very precariously, your entire life is really on the line, on this thin little wire. And there are four or five guys on the other side of the cable who are holding on to your life. And these poor guys are running around trying to make you fly. And if one of them trips, it's quite a nasty little experience for you. And wires have been known to break." It's a chilling testimony to the bravery of martial arts stunt actors. The tradeoff for such risk is beautiful, graceful artistry, like an airborne ballet.

Yeoh had to work hard to learn these kinds of stunt skills for the period films *Tai Chi Master* in 1993, *Wing Chun* in 1994, and *The Soong Sisters* in 1997. In *Crouching Tiger, Hidden Dragon,* Yeoh performed in some amazing tree-hopping fighting scenes. They were graceful and thrilling to watch. Learning how to work on wires was hard, but it paid off: Her talent garnered her a lot of attention and boosted her career even more.

dream—and Yeoh's future—was
thrown into doubt.

Yeoh was concerned that if she
didn't get back to work quickly, she
might be replaced by another actor.
Director Lee was willing to wait it
out, but only for so long. Because
the film's producers had contracts to
get all the shooting done within a
certain period of time, Yeoh had just
under three months to get back on
her feet.

Yeoh called friends at the Johns
Hopkins University of Medicine in
Baltimore, Maryland. Four days
after her injury, she met with Andy
Cosgarea, the assistant director of
Johns Hopkins's sports medicine
division and an associate professor
in the department of orthopedic
surgery. His team opted for a very
fast-track approach. Most people

The fight scenes in *Crouching Tiger, Hidden Dragon,* for which Michelle Yeoh *(right)* did many of the stunts, are some of the most spectacular ever filmed.

couldn't recover in three months, but most people aren't Michelle Yeoh.

Outpatient surgery was performed ten days after her injury, once she had regained nearly normal knee motion. After the operation, Yeoh was placed in a knee immobilizer, and within just one week, she was able to bear her full weight. Ever the professional, she came in for rehabilitation the day after her operation, although rehab doesn't usually start until a week or so after surgery. She stayed in Baltimore for three weeks and was in physical therapy every day. The surgical and rehabilitation team never had to motivate her; in fact, one of her doctors said he spent more time trying to slow her down.

Yeoh worked to strengthen her muscles and to control her swelling.

Michelle Yeoh was sensitive yet strong in her touching performance as Yu Shu Lien in *Crouching Tiger, Hidden Dragon*.

The journey back from an injury is long and painful. To regain her strength, Yeoh had physical therapy for an hour to an hour and a half each day, five to six days a week. She was able to return to a demanding shooting schedule on the set in Beijing just three months after the injury. The injury had

Michelle Yeoh (*right*) displays one of the four awards won by *Crouching Tiger, Hidden Dragon* during the 2001 Orange British Academy Film Awards in London.

threatened not only her role in *Crouching Tiger, Hidden Dragon,* but her career. However, when you're a Hong Kong action-film star, injury comes with the territory.

Chapter 6

Continuing to Break New Ground

Yes, *Madam!* was the movie that launched Michelle Yeoh's career, but it also represented a somewhat monumental step forward for Hong Kong action movies and the women starring in them. It was the first time in Hong Kong cinema history that a woman had asserted herself onscreen as a fighter and performed her own stunts. "When we came out with it, we thought, 'Well, the women will like it.' We were confident that the women would not turn their backs on us. But the most amazing thing was that the men loved it. The men were the ones who dragged their girlfriends," Yeoh said. At the age of twenty-two, she was already breaking new ground.

Blazing a Trail for Women

As one of the most-watched actresses in Asia, and now a Hollywood star, Yeoh is aware of the impact she has had on her audiences over her sixteen-year career. Her choice to do her own stunts created new opportunities for other actresses in Hong Kong action films.

The role of women in Hong Kong action cinema has changed in recent years. When Yeoh first got

Michelle Yeoh signs autographs in Beverly Hills, California.

into the business, it was more male-dominated. Now, there are more Asian movies in which the female characters are stronger and more independent. Women are also increasingly being portrayed as fighters. This is due in large part to Michelle Yeoh, who demanded more action at a time when action movie actresses did not do their own stunts.

Yeoh is something of a role model for millions of young girls. Because she does her own stunts, she is viewed as a superhero. Young girls see her flying through the air and fighting bad guys, and they realize they can be assertive and strong, too. She also lets men know that women can be tough.

Yeoh supports a number of charitable causes. She has worked

Michelle Yeoh *(left)* poses with actress Bai Ling at the premiere party for *Crouching Tiger, Hidden Dragon* in Beverly Hills, California.

with the Hong Kong Cancer Fund for many years. She also works on behalf of people with AIDS, and is a patron of the Kelly Support Group, which works with troubled teenagers. Yeoh was awarded an honorary title in Malaysia. She became a Datuk, a title similar to knight, which is the second-highest title that can be conferred by anyone other than Malaysia's king. The honor came from Sultan Azlan Shah, ruler of Malaysia's northern Perak State where Yeoh was born. Yeoh, who traveled from China to Perak to accept the title, said she was excited and honored. "This award is an acknowledgment for my achievement and my career and it will encourage me to strive further in the future," Yeoh said.

Plans for the Future

Although Yeoh would like to do more action films, she also may consider doing a comedy to further broaden her appeal. No matter what films she pursues, she will be careful to choose a quality project. She does not want to focus only on action, but wants to develop different skills and hidden talents. Drama and comedy would be new paths for her to test.

Yeoh will continue performing stunts in Hong Kong action films. But after sixteen years in show business, she has more ambitious plans. She loves the entertainment industry and wants to do more than just act. She is hoping to go behind the scenes and become a producer. In August 2000, she started her own film production company, called Mythical Films. Producers are involved with movies from the ground up: they have an idea, and from nothing they work to put it all together.

What attracted her to producing is the idea of pursuing whatever film concepts she finds interesting. "As an actress, normally you wait for the projects to come to you," she said. "But as a producer, you go out and you talk to directors and writers. That's very time-consuming and exhausting—but challenging."

ames Murdoch, chairman and CEO of Star TV,
pplauds Michelle Yeoh at a licensing agreement
igning ceremony between Media Asia and Star TV.

Mythical's first film will be called *The Touch*. Yeoh will both produce and act, which is no small feat. The movie will have a budget of $12 million. Again breaking new ground, she will be the first actress in Asia to produce a movie and act in it at the same time.

Yeoh expects Mythical to produce at least three pictures in 2001 and 2002; the company will have a budget of approximately $20 million a year. Mythical has already signed a five-year deal to make movies with Media Asia Group. Yeoh will not star in all of Mythical's films and has no intention of tailoring them specifically to herself.

She also wants Mythical to find and nurture, or help grow, the next generation of filmmakers, especially producers and young directors.

"New blood is important for any industry," she said. "It's very exciting for me right now, and for me I really believe in the talent of Asians in front of the camera and behind the scenes and in the quality of Asian cinema," she said. Yeoh's company also will work with the government of Hong Kong to set up a fund to identify Asian screenwriters and directors with potential. "Because they are the future of our industry and we have to give them the confidence, experience and exposure, as well as a job that they can make a living out of," she told *Variety*. "With Mythical Films, what we want to do is to give opportunities to the next generation of filmmakers and nurture young directors, writers, artists and all those who work behind the camera."

Back Forward Stop Refresh Home AutoFill Print

Address: @ http://owl.usc.edu/~hding/Movie/touch.html

@ Live Home Page @ Apple Computer @ Apple Support @ Apple Store @ MSN

Favorites History Search Scrapbook Page Holder

The Tou

(In Production

Producer: Michelle Yeoh

Internet zone

The Potala Palace
The Potala Palace, an administrative, religious and political complex, is built on the Red Mountain in the centre of the Lhasa valley, at an altitude of 3700 metres (above 12,000 feet). The complex comprises the White Palace and the Red Palace, with their

Front from left: Peter Pau, Thomas Chung, Michelle, Ben Chaplin. Lhasa. (SUN)

Local machine zone

Michelle Yeoh makes her debut as a movie producer with *The Touch*, in which she also stars.

She may have gone Hollywood with *Tomorrow Never Dies* and *Crouching Tiger, Hidden Dragon*, but Yeoh would like to stay in Hong Kong and do more Asian films. "I am a bit sentimental in the sense that Hong Kong is where I was first given my opportunity," she said. She hopes there will be more interaction and collaboration between the Hong Kong cinema community and Hollywood.

"What's very dear to me is that I want to make movies with Chinese talent and Chinese themes, and to either have joint East-West productions working together or an all-Asian production, and do things we can be proud of," she said.

Yeoh predicts that in the future, many Hollywood projects will be shooting in Asia, and she wants to be one of the pioneers who helps bring the two together. "Because there's so much talent, and so much landscape to shoot over in the East, and there's a lot of interest out there. And to have the American technology, the funds, and all that, to go over to Asia and expose all the Asian talent I think would be a very, very good thing."

Filmography

Owl vs. Dumbo (1984)

Twinkle Twinkle Lucky Stars (1985)

Yes Madam! (1985)

In the Line of Duty (1986) (also distributed as *Royal Warriors*)

Easy Money (1987)

Magnificent Warriors (1987)

Police Story 3: Super Cop (1992)

The Heroic Trio (1992)

Butterfly & Sword (1993)

Executioners (1993)

Holy Weapon (1993)

Once a Cop (1993)
(also distributed as *Police Story 4*)

Tai Chi Master (1993) (also distributed
as *Twin Warriors*)

Wing Chun (1994)

Wonder Seven (1994)

Shaolin Popey II: Messy Temple (1994)

*Ah Kam: The Story of a
Stuntwoman* (1996)

Tomorrow Never Dies (1997)

The Soong Sisters (1997)

Jackie Chan: My Story (1998)

Moonlight Express (1999)

Crouching Tiger, Hidden Dragon (2000)

Glossary

anterior cruciate ligament (ACL)
Ligament that stabilizes the knee joint.
A knee with an anterior cruciate
ligament injury will usually be swollen
and tender.

blockbuster Something, such as a film or
book, that sustains widespread
popularity and achieves enormous sales.

breakthrough Major achievement or
success that permits further progress,
such as in a person's career.

cameo appearance Small role in a movie or
television show, usually just one scene;
often performed by a well-known actor.

choreographer One who arranges
and directs the movements of a
dance number.

debut   First public appearance of
a performer.

drag   Dressed up as a member of the
opposite sex.

entrepreneur   Person who organizes,
operates, and assumes the risk for a
business venture.

footage   Shot or series of shots of a
specified nature or subject.

gross   Total amount of money a movie
makes before anyone takes a cut.
"Low-grossing" would be a movie that
made little money or lost money.

microfilm   Film on which printed
materials are photographed at a very
small size to make them easy to store.

mime   Dramatic art of portraying
characters and acting out situations
using gestures and body movements
without speaking; pantomime.

outpatient surgery   Operation after
which a person does not spend the
night in a hospital, but instead is
released to go home.

period piece   Any work of art whose
special value lies in its portrayal of a
historical period.

producer   Person who supervises and controls the finances, creation, and public presentation of a play, film, program, or other work.

set   Staging of a movie where the action and dialogue are filmed.

shoot   To record a scene of a movie on film.

stage name   Name used by an actor instead of his or her real name.

traction   To immobilize an injured part of the body to enable it to heal.

vertebra   One of the bony segments that make up the spine.

upstage   To distract attention from another performer or to force him or her out of the spotlight.

wire work   Using wires to suspend a stuntperson in midair, giving the illusion of flight or levitation.

For More Information

Web Sites

HK Action Films.com
http://www.hkactionfilms.com

Internet Movie Database
http://us.imdb.com/Name?Yeoh,+
  Michelle

The Michelle Yeoh Webring
http://owl.usc.edu/~hding/yeohring

Year of the Tiger
http://www.geocities.com/foodog42/
  biography2

For Further Reading

Bordwell, David. *Planet Hong Kong: Popular Cinema and the Art of Entertainment*. Cambridge, MA: Harvard University Press, 2000.

Fu, Poshek, and David Desser. *The Cinema of Hong Kong: History, Arts, Identity*. New York: Cambridge University Press, 2000.

Hammond, Stefan (foreword by Michelle Yeoh). *Hollywood East: Hong Kong Movies and the People Who Made Them*. Chicago: Contemporary Books, 2000.

Hammond, Stefan, and Mike Wilkins. *Sex and Zen and a Bullet in the Head: The Essential Guide to Hong Kong's Mind-Bending Films.* New York: Simon & Schuster Trade, 1996.

Logan, Bey. *Hong Kong Action Cinema.* Woodstock, NY: Overlook Press, 1996.

Lu, Sheldon Hsia-peng, ed., and Hsiao-Peng Lu. *Transnational Chinese Cinemas: Identity, Nationhood, Gender.* Honolulu: University of Hawaii Press, 1997.

Stokes, Lisa Odham. *City on Fire: Hong Kong Cinema.* New York: Verso, 1999.

Teo, Stephen. *Hong Kong Cinema: The Extra Dimensions.* British Film Institute, 1998.

Yau, Esther C.M. *At Full Speed: Hong Kong Cinema in a Borderless*

World. Minneapolis, MN: University of Minnesota Press, 2001.

Works Cited

Accomando, Beth. "The Wrath of Khan." *Giant Robot,* Issue 7. http://www.giantrobot.com/issues/issue07/khan/khanmain.html

Cheng, Scarlet. "007's Sidekick: A Different Leading Lady." *The Los Angeles Times*, December 1997.

Greene, Ray. "Hong Kong Action Queen Michelle Yeoh Gets a Leg up on the Competition in the New James Bond Flick *Tomorrow Never Dies*." Mr. Showbiz.com http://mrshowbiz.go.com/celebrities/interviews/392_2.html

Hochman, David. "Ladies Who Launch." *Entertainment Weekly*, September 21, 1997.
htp://www.ew.com/ew/features/971121/action_actress/my2.html

Keeter, Nicole. "The Story of Yeoh." *Time Out New York*, December 2000.

Kwong, Kevin. "Action Star Gets New Footing" *Variety*, August 21, 2000.

Reid, Craig. "Crouching Tiger, Hidden Dragon: Michelle Yeoh." Cinescape.com, December 21, 2000.
http://www.cinescape.com/0/Editorial.asp?aff_id=0&this_cat=Movies&action=page&obj_id=17602

"StudioLA's Suzanne Kai Interviews Michelle Yeoh," March 2001.
http://www.studiola.com/interviews/michelle_yeoh.html

Yips, Jeff. "The Show Must Go On." *Orthopedic Technology Review.* Volume 3, Number 1, January/February 2001.
http://www.orthopedictechreview.com/issues/janfeb01/pg16.htm

Index

About the Author

Nancy L. Stair is a writer and editor who lives in Greenwich Village, New York City, with her sweetheart, Charley, a professional trombone player.

Photo Credits

Cover, pp. 22, 35, 40, 50–51, 57, 60–61, 69, 74–75, 77 © The Everett Collection; pp. 4, 78, 82, 88–89 © AFP/Corbis; p. 10 © Kin Cheung/Timepix; pp. 26–27, 65, 92 © AP/Wide World Photos; pp. 46, 54 © Mitchell Gerber/Corbis; p. 85 © Reuters NewMedia Inc./Corbis; pp. 92–93 © www.owl.usc.edu.

Series Design and Layout

Les Kanturek